UNYIELDING FLOODS

UNYIELDING FLOODS

Peter Caton

Dewi Lewis Publishing

To my Mother and Father,

and to the courageous people of South Sudan,

who endure the rising waters with strength and dignity.

As a documentary photographer for over twenty-five years, I've had the privilege to work alongside countless media outlets and organisations worldwide to document global humanitarian and environmental crises. But it is the profound impact of climate change in South Sudan that has brought me to this book. Over the past four years, I have been chronicling an ever-deepening humanitarian crisis. A crisis that has displaced millions of South Sudanese and devastated entire communities. In these photographs, you will not find still rivers or gentle rain, but water unbound, surging across plains, blurring the lines between land and water.

My story with South Sudan began in January 2020, and in the most unusual way. I was visiting my family in North Yorkshire, and we were attending Sunday Service at the local church. The congregation rose in unison for a hymn, and I opened the book in front of me. There, mysteriously tucked between the pages, was a tiny paper flag. Perplexed, I slowly turned it over, and printed on the back were the words 'South Sudan'. Despite many years of working across Africa, the world's newest country remained uncharted territory for me.

I returned to Africa for commissions, and that curious moment in church remained quietly etched in my memory. Shortly afterwards, the world was plunged into the COVID-19 pandemic, and I found myself stranded in East Africa. Months of uncertainty followed – until suddenly I began to receive a wave of requests from humanitarian organisations in South Sudan. I couldn't help but feel that something was aligning.

I accepted a commission to photograph the COVID-19 response for 'Action Against Hunger' in South Sudan. Home to eleven million people, this East African country was still scarred by years of civil war. But a new crisis was emerging: relentless floods, driven by unusually heavy rains amplified by climate change. The White Nile overflowed across the vast Sudd wetlands, swallowing entire communities and erasing fertile land.

The Charity's Country Director asked me to urgently stop what I was doing and take a charter flight into the heart of the disaster zone. From the air, a remote town called Old Fangak resembled a cluster of islands; the floods had ravaged what was once land.

In Old Fangak, there are no roads; the only means of transport is by canoe. I arrived at the first location, an abandoned school, which had been transformed into an emergency refuge for families forced to flee their homes. Classrooms once filled with kids eager to learn were now home to grieving families fervently praying with fears for survival (pages 14-15). At that moment, I began to understand the significance of that fragile paper flag, found in a tiny church far away in North Yorkshire.

What followed became the heart of this book. It is not only a photographic documentation of a land devastated by climate change – it is a testament to the quiet dignity of the South Sudanese and their collective endeavours to create hope in the face of unimaginable adversity.

Organisations, such as 'Action Against Hunger' or 'Médecins Sans Frontières', were already on the ground – struggling against the brutal challenges of combating a landscape being entirely rewritten. The unprecedented scale of the crisis overwhelmed their courageous efforts. Vast areas of South Sudan cut off by rising waters had become almost entirely inaccessible. Floating grass islands blocked routes along the White Nile in flood-ravaged Jonglei State. A football pitch in Old Fangak, once used as a landing zone for UN helicopters delivering emergency aid, was now completely submerged.

Yet in the face of these tribulations, I witnessed the most extraordinary display of unity and determination. Using salvaged buckets and their bare hands, communities worked tirelessly around the clock to protect what was left of their land – dykes were built around the football pitch using mud. People fought back against the water to keep the landing zone intact so UN helicopters could continue delivering emergency aid (pages 70-71).

In vulnerable areas, locals volunteer to patrol villages day and night with firearms ready to alert the community if a dam bursts. The piercing sound of gunshots echoing in the night jolts you awake, reminding you that the threat is constant and unforgiving.

A memorable photograph, I captured towards the end of my first trip, was of a community forced to relocate to a small elevated area called 'Highlands' (page 31). I politely asked if the residents could stand beside their remaining mound of salvaged sorghum (millet). All their crops had washed away, their livestock drowned or perished from waterborne diseases. With no other food source within a close radius, starvation loomed as an imminent and alarming threat.

By the time I returned the following year, news had quickly spread throughout Old Fangak and its neighbouring villages – and even in the remotest of areas, I was met with a heartfelt welcome. Driven by a powerful desire for the visibility of their plight, people were eager to come forward and become part of a collective effort, sharing personal stories of their lives, their losses, and their resilience.

The severe malnutrition I'd feared became a bleak reality. In a desperate bid to stave off hunger amongst communities, also fighting rife diseases such as malaria, people had turned to collecting water lily bulbs – wading chest high through crocodile-infested waters, heavy green stems wrapped around their necks. Low in nutritional value, even an entire sack of bulbs ground into a paste would barely yield enough to feed one person, let alone a whole family (pages 53-59).

With a heavy heart, after months in the field, I was preparing to depart Old Fangak for a second time when the local Head of Base for 'Action Against Hunger' asked me to join him. He pointed towards flooded fields in the distance. He said, "When you return next year, all of this will be rice paddies." I looked at him with surprise. Rice farming was not practised in this region, and his words seemed to stem only from optimism rather than anything realistically achievable.

Upon returning to South Sudan for a third year in October 2022, I was stunned to see a vibrant green sea of rice fields. During my absence, the charity had initiated an empowering women-only pilot project to teach agricultural rice-growing techniques in floodwater, which was in turn shared with their husbands to offer a solution to fend off hunger (pages 92–97).

The rice fields represented the first real glimmer of hope; the locals rejoiced in their success. I helped develop a multimedia presentation with 'Action Against Hunger' for this incredible innovation. It was presented to the government in the capital city of Juba, and the project was implemented in flood-prone areas across the country. Presently, it continues to transform the lives and well-being of farming families and their communities.

Adaptation became the only means of survival. Isolated communities developed other ingenious ways to endure by using layers of tall grass that thrive in flooded areas to craft floating pontoons designed to rise and fall with the floodwaters (pages 96–97). Villagers dismantled their old homes to cleverly repurpose the timber to rebuild new homes on the floating platforms (page 88). People began to feel a rare sense of stability amidst the chaos.

As record water levels in Lake Victoria, Africa's largest fresh water lake, flow downstream through the Nile, experts claim South Sudan may represent the first mass displacement due to climate change. During a final visit in 2024, I visited Malakal, in the Upper Nile State, and I witnessed a dam burst. A frantic effort followed to contain the rushing water (pages 110 & 120). Unfortunately, yet another village was lost (pages 106-107 & 118). In other cases, elevated areas once considered safe, like 'Highlands', had become uninhabitable, overrun by venomous snakes and fire ants. Most populations in flood-affected areas now live aboard makeshift grass pontoons, adjusting to an escalating reality.

One question I regularly asked people photographed in this book is: *"If you had the chance to leave and live in an Internally Displaced Person (IDP) camp in the capital, Juba, would you go?"* Without exception, the dignified response of the villagers was that they would never leave their land and surrender it to the water – the land is their identity, and the only place they have ever known.

'Unyielding Floods' bears testament to the real lives of these real people – and to the collective resilience of the human spirit in the face of unrelenting hardship. It remains the defining theme of my years in South Sudan, and a source of lasting inspiration. The camera cannot solve what it captures, but it can bear witness. The book in your hands is both a record and a call to see, care, and remember that for many, the floods never truly recede.

Peter Caton
July 2025

“It all started in June and because of that we couldn't harvest our crops. They were all washed away with the floods.”

Nyayua Thang

*"I have been throwing water over the dyke all day.
I got tired. I couldn't stand up anymore."*

Nyakoang Mayieh

P5
CLASS P5
P5

"I am an old man. With these legs I will not manage to move through the water too far."

Peter Kak

"We don't fit inside (the school), that's why the bed is outside. We sleep in the open."

Mother and daughter,
Nyagout Lok and Nyakoang Majok

"We make a sacrifice to bring our children to safety using a bucket."

Nyalong Wal

"The worst part of this flood is losing everything. My mat, mosquito net, bed sheets, and clothes were all taken by the water. Now, I rely on the river for sustenance. If I can catch a fish, I eat; if not, I go hungry."

Nyakeet Yuay

Scooter

"We are surrounded everywhere by water, and we have nowhere to run to. People are dying of hunger and the floods are to blame."

Nyakeak Rambon

"I planted maize next to my home, but when the second flood came, it destroyed it. I didn't even get to harvest it. I feel sad because, before these floods, I had a kitchen garden that put food on the table."

Nyadiang Gak

"I'm feeling ill because these floods make my body hurt."

Nyadieng Riok

"I'm not happy because I throw water out every day. I'm not going to school because I'm throwing this water over the dyke."

Nyakueni Both

“We lost everything in the floods but we do not want to leave this place. We have lived here all our lives and call this place home.”

Nyatoya Mawich

“We are happy and even laughing while we work, because this rice will be our survival.”

Nyanguat Lep

P 6
KO.
ONELOVE
P.6

IKB

"The flood occurred last night while we were all asleep. It left our property destroyed, and all our food has gone apart from some maize."

Nyarur Bamgout

Peter Caton is an award-winning British photographer from Scarborough, Yorkshire. Passionately committed to documenting humanitarian causes, he has lived on the road with a suitcase and a camera bag in the developing world since 2006.

His powerful Hasselblad images have been featured in numerous international publications and dedicated exhibitions, and the series 'Unyielding Floods' has earned multiple awards, including first place in the 2021 International Photography Awards' environmental category.

In humanising South Sudan's climate change statistics, the series has helped spotlight the disaster and has fuelled advocacy, funding, and practical support for local communities.

www.petercaton.com

I would like to express my deepest gratitude to everyone who contributed to the making of this book.

Special thanks to **Action Against Hunger** and **International Medical Corps** for their invaluable assistance with access throughout the fieldwork; to **Susan Martinez**, for her tireless work conducting field interviews and writing essays that gave further depth to these stories; to **Philip Vaughan**, for his generous mentorship and guidance throughout this journey; to **Kieran Bell**, for his exceptional promotional and post production support; to my family, for their constant and unconditional support through every stage of this project; and to **Dallas Jay Hunter**, for her inspiration and encouragement in helping make this book a reality.

Without the dedication and support of each of you, this work would not have been possible.

The generosity of all our Kickstarter supporters is very much appreciated. In particular we would like to acknowledge the following people.

Kathy & Len Abline
Gideon Don Adlon
Jay Arce
Lou Arce
Luis M. Arce
Patsy Agpalza, LCSW
Christian Alderson
Claudio Andreoletti
Robert Ashby
Adrien Auzanneau
Brooke & Gage Beauchemin
Conrad Birch
Jenny Biss
Carsten ten Brink
Tom Broadbent
Steven Brown
Browns Caravan Park
Alexis Budda
Stephen Burnett
Alan Cameron
David Carrier
John & Pam Caton
Bill Cleveland
Michael Cockerham
Tim Cox
Robert Coleman
Sarah Collett
Tony Craven
David Curtis
Brenda Cutler
Lizzy Dahl
Roland Degner
Peter Dench
Luke Duggleby
Dave Dunn-Birch
Tom Elkins
Reinhardt Euler
Angela Fedak
Vince Ferraro
Emma Fewster
Jorge Fortuna
Alison Freebairn
Adrian Griffiths
Mary Hassan
Chris Havard
Jean & Frank Havard
Erik Hinz
Brenda Hooper
Dallas Jay Hunter
David Hurd
Ryan Jaeger
Annette James
Robert Janovski
Carol Johnson
Christine Joiner
Lynda Kershaw
Sarah Khan
Kristopher Kneen
France Leclerc
LeeSun, Self Love Roadmap
Alison Leigh
Mike Leigh
Dave Littler
C. Liu
Margaret Lloyd
Sue Louth
John Lyon
Amanda Macey
Donald Maciver
Katy Marsh-Davies
Margaret H. McAdams
David Metson
Isa Miah & family
Neil A. Miller
Edouard Monfrais

Frederic Monpeat
Glenn Morris
Stephen Murray
John Myers
Gary Nicol
John Oxley
Jeff Del Papa
Jerome De Perlinghi
Kevin E. G. Perry
Mark Phillips
Jonathan Robinson
Patricia Russell
Scargill Movement
Denis Santoro
Walter Sedriks
David Shaw
Amy Siciliani
Michael Sloan
Colin Spink
David St.Clair
Stephen & Fia Swalwell
James Tagg
Thomas Tauscher
Stephen Robert Thornton
Liz Tite
Pia Uhlenberg
Christiana Vater
Gary Weekes
Deborah Ruth Welford
Isaiah Whisner
Phil White
John Wilson
Sally-ann Wilson

We would also like to thank the sponsors of the campaign

First published in the UK in 2025 by

Dewi Lewis Publishing
8, Broomfield Road
Heaton Moor
Stockport SK4 4ND
England

www.dewilewis.com

ISBN: 978-1-9169915-17-6

Design: Dewi Lewis
Print: EBS, Verona, Italy